This book is intentionally blank

This book is intentionally blank

This book is intentionally blank

This book is intentionally blank

This book is intentionally blank

This book is intentionally blank

This book is intentionally blank

This book is intentionally blank

This book is intentionally blank

This book is intentionally blank

This book is intentionally blank

This book is intentionally blank

This book is intentionally blank

This book is intentionally blank

This book is intentionally blank

This book is intentionally blank

This book is intentionally blank

This book is intentionally blank

This book is intentionally blank

This book is intentionally blank

This book is intentionally blank

This book is intentionally blank

This book is intentionally blank

This book is intentionally blank

This book is intentionally blank

This book is intentionally blank

This book is intentionally blank

This book is intentionally blank

This book is intentionally blank

This book is intentionally blank

This book is intentionally blank

This book is intentionally blank

This book is intentionally blank

This book is intentionally blank

This book is intentionally blank

This book is intentionally blank

This book is intentionally blank

This book is intentionally blank

This book is intentionally blank

This book is intentionally blank

This book is intentionally blank

This book is intentionally blank

This book is intentionally blank

This book is intentionally blank

This book is intentionally blank

This book is intentionally blank

This book is intentionally blank

This book is intentionally blank

This book is intentionally blank

This book is intentionally blank

This book is intentionally blank

This book is intentionally blank

This book is intentionally blank

This book is intentionally blank

This book is intentionally blank

This book is intentionally blank

This book is intentionally blank

This book is intentionally blank

This book is intentionally blank

This book is intentionally blank

This book is intentionally blank

This book is intentionally blank

This book is intentionally blank

This book is intentionally blank

This book is intentionally blank

This book is intentionally blank

This book is intentionally blank

This book is intentionally blank

This book is intentionally blank

This book is intentionally blank

This book is intentionally blank

This book is intentionally blank

This book is intentionally blank

This book is intentionally blank

This book is intentionally blank

This book is intentionally blank

This book is intentionally blank

This book is intentionally blank

This book is intentionally blank

This book is intentionally blank

This book is intentionally blank

This book is intentionally blank

This book is intentionally blank

This book is intentionally blank

This book is intentionally blank

This book is intentionally blank

This book is intentionally blank

This book is intentionally blank

This book is intentionally blank

This book is intentionally blank

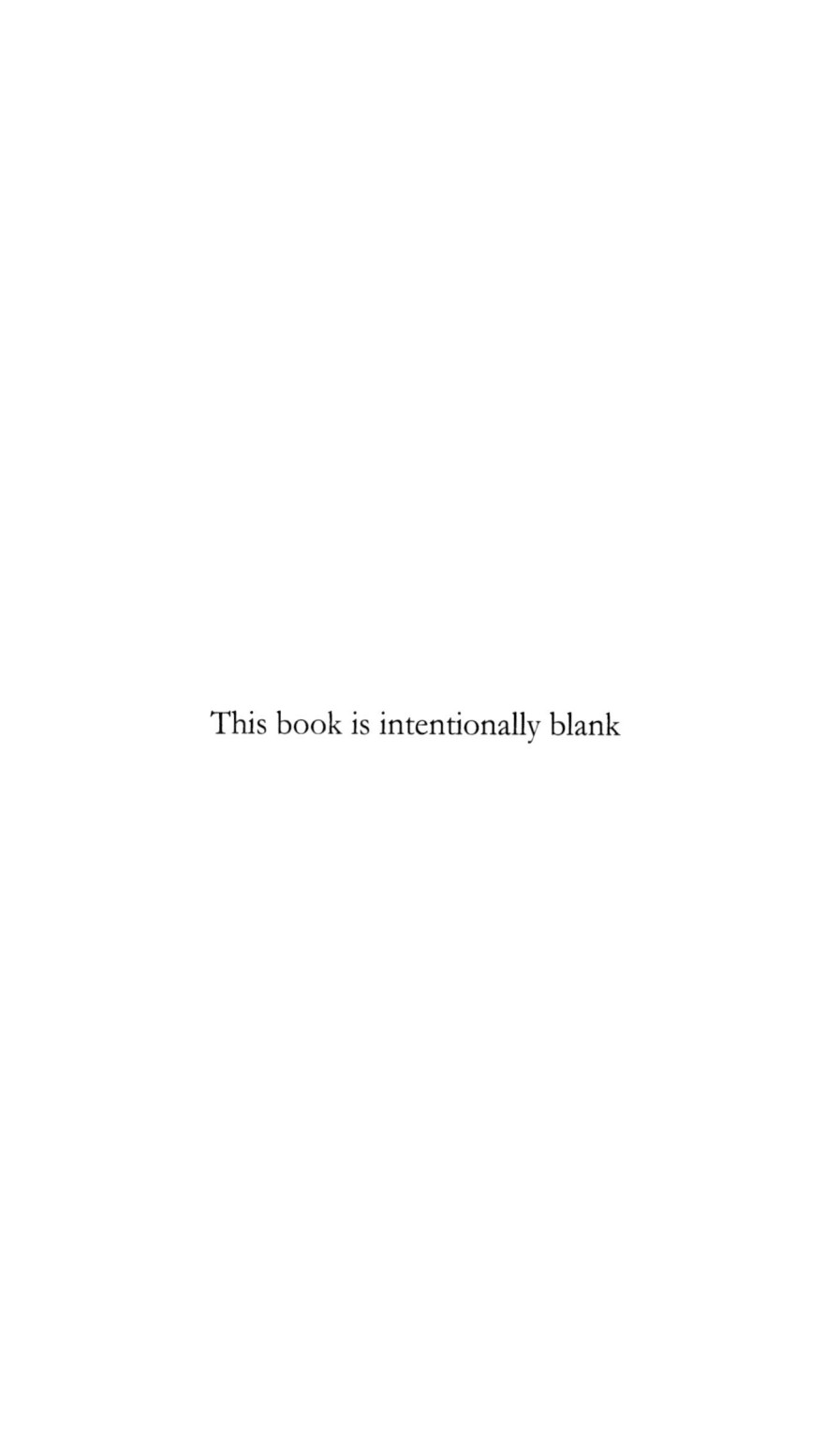

This book is intentionally blank

This book is intentionally blank

This book is intentionally blank

This book is intentionally blank

This book is intentionally blank

This book is intentionally blank

This book is intentionally blank

This book is intentionally blank

This book is intentionally blank

This book is intentionally bl

c

CPSIA information can be obtained at www.ICGtesting.com
Printed in the USA
LVOW08s1034031114

411773LV00009B/101/P

9 781494 774165